COURAGEOUS HEART

BIBLE STUDY FOR WOMEN SERIES

(BOOK 2)

Kimberly Taylor

TakeBackYourTemple.com

Cover Image by:

www.iStockphoto.com

Table of Contents

Introduction

Thank you for starting this second book of the *Bible Study for Women* series, *Courageous Heart*. In this 4-week study, you will learn life-changing principles from the bible, specifically about how four women demonstrated courage in tough situations: Abigail, Deborah, Rahab, and Esther.

Why is courage important? It takes courage to affect *change*. Whether you are in a position of leadership, engaged in conflict, or seeking to save lives, you have the choice to accept things as they are or work to change them.

If you make the second choice, you may face opposition. In some cases, the opposition may be the loss of a relationship; in the case of most of the women in this study, the opposition could have resulted in the loss of life: Theirs!

What would drive someone to seek to change a situation, knowing that doing so could possibly result in her death? Usually, courage comes about when the situation challenges a deeply held value such as:

- Seeking justice
- Doing the right thing
- Preserving your own life
- Saving an entire race of people

The situations we face may not be as dramatic as those we'll learn about in the bible study, but when it is time to demonstrate courage, we must be able to draw upon our source.

The source of our courage as Christians today is found in the following scripture:

> "Have I not commanded you? Be strong and courageous. Do not be terrified; do not be discouraged, for the LORD your God will be with you wherever you go. (Joshua 1:9)"

We know that change can be scary. But God himself says that the reason we do not need to be afraid or discouraged is that He will be with you. God's presence is the source of our courage.

I think the ultimate trait of a woman with a courageous heart is a "finisher's heart." That is a woman who is committed to finishing what she set out to do - no matter the cost.

My pastor recently preached a sermon called "D.N.F." He recounted the story of Morgan Uceny, the young track and field runner who competed in the 2012 London Olympic games. During the 1500 meter race, Morgan had the misfortune to fall when her leg contacted the foot of the runner in front of her.

The world watched as Morgan, completely heartbroken, pounded the pavement in tears. And she stayed down in defeat. In the end, she left the track not having finished the race. The board that should have recorded her finishing time instead showed "D.N.F," which means "Did Not Finish."

Our pastor exhorted us to adopt a new motto in our race to finish well in this life. Instead of "Did Not Finish," let our motto become **"Did Not Faint."**

To remember this, I recall the story of another Olympian, Derek Redmond in the 1992 Barcelona games. Derek stumbled too in his race. But here is the difference between Derek and Morgan.

Derek got **up**.

He energized the crowd by his courageous attempt to finish the race, even if he had to hobble to do it.

Then suddenly, a man appeared out of the crowd. This man came alongside Derek to hold him up and help him finish the race.

That man was his **Father**.

The next time you are faced with a situation in which courage is needed, take the time to consider the mightiness of your God. Remember that you are not alone. **Focus on your Father.**

God assures us in Isaiah 41:10: "Fear not, for I am with you; Be not dismayed, for I am your God. I will strengthen you, Yes, I will help you, I will uphold you with My righteous right hand." Hold on to that promise and don't let go.

Now, because you are reading a bible study, I assume that you already have a relationship with God through accepting Jesus Christ as your Savior. But just in case my assumption is wrong, I'd like to give you a resource about establishing a relationship with God through Jesus Christ. You can also use this resource if you want to re-dedicate your life to Christ:

http://www.everystudent.com/features/gettingc onnected.html

Are you ready to learn more about how women demonstrated courage in the bible? Let's get started!

How to Get the Most from this Study

The aim for each study in the *Bible Study for Women* series is to keep it simple. I want the lessons in the bible to change your life. To that end, it should be helpful to know how the lessons are organized and what you need to make the most of your study time.

Within each week's lesson, you will find:

- *Focus Scriptures* to memorize related to the current topic

- *Lesson Insight* that discusses the week's story in depth

- *Speak the WORD* affirmations that confirm your identity in Christ

- *Aim for Change* that provides questions for further reflection and discussion

To start the study, you need to have:

- *A bible:* I recommend the *New King James Version* or the *New American Standard Bible* for readability. I believe that it is important to use a bible translation that you understand for private study.

- *Index cards:* These will come in handy to write focus scriptures on so that you can 'feed' on them throughout the day.

- *A small notebook or journal:* This will enable you to keep track of the blessings/lessons you are learning as a result of this study.

- *A heart and mind that is open to the Holy Spirit's teaching:* One of the Holy Spirit's roles in the believer's life is that of *Teacher* (John 14:26). Invite Him through prayer to show you plainly the lesson God wants to teach you before you begin each study session. Be attentive to the still small voice within that prompts you to take action on the word you are learning about.

- *A commitment and willingness to give yourself grace:* If you find yourself forgetting to study as you planned, don't beat yourself up. Just start your study where you left off at your next opportunity. Think "forward motion" and keep going!

Week 1: Courage in Leadership (Deborah)

Focus Scripture

> "...But let those who love Him be like the sun When it comes out in full strength."

- Judges 5:31

Lesson Insight

If there was ever a strong woman in the bible, it was Deborah. Deborah is the only documented female judge in the bible (see Judges, Chapter 4). The term "Judge" in the bible has a slightly different meaning than it does today.

In addition to presiding over legal matters, a biblical judge often assumed the role of "deliverer," providing military leadership to deliver the children of Israel from their enemies.

If you read the book of Judges, you'll see why a deliverer was needed. In almost every chapter of the book, the same depressing cycle repeated over and over:

1. The children of Israel did evil in the sight of the Lord
2. The Lord delivered them into the hands of an enemy
3. The children of Israel cried out to the Lord for deliverance
4. The Lord in His compassion raised up a Judge to deliver the people
5. After deliverance and a few years of obedience, the people once again did evil in the sight of the Lord...

During Deborah's time, the enemy into whose hands the Israelites had fallen was the King of Canaan, Jabin. Jabin, along with the commander of his army Sisera, had oppressed the Israelites harshly for 20 years.

However, the children of Israel cried out to the Lord for deliverance. He responded with a message to Deborah (who in addition to Judge was also a Prophetess and wife), explaining how the deliverance would be accomplished.

The message involved enlisting Barak, a leader of the tribe of Naphtali. Deborah sent for him and when Barak came to her, she told him God's plan:

> "Has not the Lord God of Israel commanded, 'Go and deploy troops at Mount Tabor; take with you ten thousand men of the sons of Naphtali and of the sons of Zebulun; and against you I will deploy Sisera, the commander of Jabin's army, with his chariots and his multitude at the River Kishon; and I will deliver him into your hand'?"

Barak listened but had a surprising request of His own: "If you will go with me, then I will go; but if you will not go with me, I will not go!"

What? Barak was a leader in position to command 10,000 men into battle. Yet he said he would not go without this woman going with him. He must have had great respect for Deborah. Think about it: How many of you would be willing to go into an active battle-zone? You might say 'no' at first, but I'll bet you would go if the lives of the people you loved were at stake.

Deborah, called later in scripture as "a mother in Israel," cared enough about her people to risk her life for them. And she clearly had great confidence that God would be true to His word and deliver the people. She answered Barak:

"I will surely go with you; nevertheless there will be no glory for you in the journey you are taking, for the Lord will sell Sisera into the hand of a woman."

Deborah and Barak did exactly what the Lord directed. With the 10,000 men under Barak's command, they positioned themselves for victory.

When Sisera heard about Barak's encampment, he gathered his troops to meet them in battle.

The two enemies clashed, but it was no contest; the bible records that the Lord defeated Sisera's troops until not one was left. In the heat of battle, there was only one thing left for Sisera to do: He got down off of his chariot and ran away.

But he picked the wrong tent in which to seek shelter. The woman who lived there, Jael, was quite welcoming on the surface; she told him not to fear. She even gave him milk and a blanket. However, when Sisera was asleep from weariness, she...drove a tent peg through his temple with a hammer, killing him. Now, that's hardcore.

A shocking end to Sisera's life for us, but it was exactly what Deborah had prophesied: The Lord sold Sisera into the hands of a woman.

So what does Deborah's story tell us about how we can exercise courage in our own lives? First, Deborah was able to recognize God's voice when she heard it. Our ability to hear His voice will grow as we spend quiet time with Him consistently.

Secondly, Deborah took action as the Lord told her to without delay. Many times when the Lord tells us to take action, delicate timing is involved. While you don't want to be hasty, once you are confident that it is the Lord telling you to move, then move!

As author and bible teacher Pastor Charles Stanley says, "Obey God and leave all the consequences to Him."

Let God be your commander and He will order your steps to bring glory and honor to Him!

Speak the WORD

Speak this affirmation out loud as often as possible, based on this week's study:

> "God, declare you are my commander today. I spend time with you, eagerly awaiting the words that you say to me. Give me the courage to obey your word. Give me the strength to persevere. In time, I will reap if I do not faint."

Aim For Change

Read Judges, Chapter 4 and then answer the following questions.

1. What leadership role did Deborah hold in Israel?

2. Why did Deborah send for Barak?

3. What reasons could Barak have had for insisting that Deborah go with him to face Sisera?

4. Why do you think Deborah did not hesitate to go with Barak?

5. How did events transpire once Barak's troops met Sisera?

6. Has there ever been a time when the Lord showed you or someone else you know a future event and things transpired according to the vision?

7. What steps will you take to listen for God's voice more clearly this week?

Week 2: Courage in Conflict (Abigail)

Focus Scripture

Strength and honor are her clothing; She shall rejoice in time to come.

She opens her mouth with wisdom, And on her tongue is the law of kindness.

- Proverbs 31:25-26

Lesson Insight

King David in the bible is known as the "sweet Psalmist of Israel." But in the episode we'll learn about this week, he wasn't so sweet. In fact, before David became king, he was such a hot-head in his anger that he was ready to kill every male in a man's household because the man wronged him.

But fortunately, he was saved from making that mistake by the quick-thinking actions of a courageous woman: Abigail (see 1 Samuel 25: 2-35).

When Abigail is first mentioned in bible (1 Samuel 25:3), it is to compare her with her husband. Abigail was described as "a woman of good understanding and beautiful appearance."

When I read that Abigail had good understanding, the scripture from Proverbs 9:10 came to mind - "The fear of the LORD is the beginning of wisdom, and the knowledge of the Holy One is understanding."

We too can be described as women of good understanding as we grow in the knowledge of God through the study and application of His word.

In contrast Abigail's husband, a rich man named Nabal, was described as "harsh and evil in his doings." Later in the chapter, the name 'Nabal' is said to mean "Fool." Who would name their child "Fool"? In Nabal's case, it was a self-fulfilling prophecy.

When I learned that Nabal means "Fool," another scripture came to mind, this one from Psalm 14:1: "...The fool has said in his heart, 'There is no God.' They are corrupt, They have done abominable works, There is none who does good."

In the account from 1 Samuel 25: 4-13, Nabal repaid evil for David's good. You see, David and his mighty men were at this time on the run, trying to evade the attempts of King Saul to kill David. However, when Nabal's shepherds encountered David's men in the wilderness, David's men provided protection for the shepherds.

However, when David sent ten of his men to Nabal to humbly ask for Nabal to supply whatever food he could spare for them, Nabal answered harshly, "Who is David, and who is the son of Jesse? There are many servants nowadays who break away each one from his master. Shall I then take my bread and my water and my meat that I have killed for my shearers, and give it to men when I do not know where they are from?"

When David heard about Nabal's response, he ordered his men to put on their swords. Four hundred men went with David, who was ready to get revenge on Nabal for the insult. That's what I meant earlier when I called David a hot-head; while David had a right to his anger, making a rash decision to kill all the males in Nabal's household was *overkill* in my opinion.

However, one of Nabal's servants went to Abigail and told her what happened, including the fact that the entire household now was in danger because of Nabal.

Without telling Nabal, Abigail took action to avoid disaster. She gathered an abundance of food and had it all loaded up on donkeys. Then she sent her servants ahead of her to meet David with the food while she followed on a donkey.

When she came upon David, she fell down before him to the ground. She said in part, "Please forgive the trespass of your maidservant. For the Lord will certainly make for my lord an enduring house, because my lord fights the battles of the Lord, and evil is not found in you throughout your days."

In examining Abigail's approach to David, I see that she appealed to David's better nature: She reminded him of his higher purpose (fighting the battles of the Lord) and of his basic character (that evil is not in him). She knew of David's destiny as the king of Israel and she spoke blessing to him, getting him to think about what he was about to do.

Surely, if David had slaughtered all the men in Nabal's household, word would have spread throughout the nation about him repaying evil for evil. David's destiny would have likely been altered for the worse.

The account shows that David listened to Abigail. He said, "Blessed is the Lord God of Israel, who sent you this day to meet me! And blessed is your advice and blessed are you, because you have kept me this day from coming to bloodshed and from avenging myself with my own hand. For indeed, as the Lord God of Israel lives, who has kept me back from hurting you, unless you had hurried and come to meet me, surely by morning light no males would have been left to Nabal!"

He received Abigail's gift and bid her to return to her house. Ten days later, the Lord struck Nabal and he died. Eventually, Abigail became David's wife.

Abigail's display of wisdom and strength in averting disaster is a lesson to us all. It shows us the power of speaking the right words at the right time, especially when those words bring light into the lives of others.

Speak the WORD

Speak this affirmation out loud as often as possible, based on this week's study:

> "Lord, thank you for molding me into a woman who respects and honors you. I look to you to

cloth me with your strength during times of weakness. Lord, I praise you for helping me to speak with wisdom towards others and operating with the law of kindness in my heart."

Aim For Change

Read 1 Samuel 25: 2-35 and then answer the following questions.

1. How did the bible contrast Abigail's character with Nabal's?

2. What request did David send his men to make to Nabal?

3. Why was David so angry that Nabal refused his request?

4. When Abigail heard about what Nabal had done, what was her response?

5. How did Abigail approach David to keep her household from danger?

6. How have you managed conflict in the past? Did you take action immediately to resolve it or ignore it?

7. Do you speak with wisdom in your dealings with others? Ask the Lord in prayer to help you speak with kindness and wisdom.

Week 3: Courage in Action (Rahab)

Focus Scripture

'...for the LORD your God is He who goes with you, to fight for you against your enemies, to save you.'

- Deuteronomy 20:4

Lesson Insight

Rahab was a woman of knowledge (see Joshua, chapter 2). Because her house was on the city wall in Jericho, she was in position to see who came into the city and who went out.

She also knew things because of her profession; Rahab was a harlot and as such, gained knowledge through the confidences shared with her.

Both types of knowledge came into play when two men came to stay at her house. You see, Joshua (Moses' successor) had sent these men to Jericho to spy. Jericho was at the border of the Promised Land, which the Lord had swore that He would give to the Israelites.

When the King of Jericho found out about the two strangers in the city, he sent to Rahab, ordering her to bring the men out. He knew about their intentions to spy.

But Rahab was crafty. She had already hidden the spies on the housetop roof, covering them with Flax stalks to conceal them. She told the men whom the king sent to her, "Yes, the men came to me, but I did not know where they were from. And it happened as the gate was being shut, when it was dark, that the men went out. Where the men went I do not know; pursue them quickly, for you may overtake them."

Rahab's lie worked. The pursuers were misdirected and went their way to continue the search. Once they were gone, Rahab brought the spies out and then explained why she had helped them: "I know that the Lord has given you the land, that the terror of you has fallen on us, and that all the inhabitants of the land are fainthearted because of you."

She further stated that the city had heard about the Israelites' battle victories up until that point. And in Rahab's mind, the decisive victories led her to one inescapable conclusion: "And as soon as we heard these things, our hearts melted; neither did there remain any more courage in anyone because of you, for the Lord your God, He is God in heaven above and on earth beneath."

It is remarkable to me that this woman, who lived in a pagan city with no regard for the God of Israel, was led to declare the greatness of Him. Rahab come to this conclusion only from hearsay. How much more can we declare His greatness because we know God through personal experience?

Because Rahab believed in the God of Israel's power, she courageously helped the spies, risking the king's men discovering her deception and the consequences of it.

In return for her help, she asked the spies to spare herself, her parents and her brothers and sisters once they had conquered the city. The spies pledged to do so.

Rahab then advised the spies to hide in the mountains for three days until the pursuers had returned back to

Jericho. Then the spies could return safely to their own camp.

They made a covenant with Rahab before they left; they asked her to bind a scarlet cord in the window and, on the day of the Israelites' invasion, to make sure that her family was inside of her house. That way, they could be safe during the battle raging outside.

When the Israelites conquered Jericho, the spies were true to their word. Rahab and her family were saved. Rahab ended up being in the lineage of two illustrious figures in the bible as recorded in Matthew 1:5:

> *Salmon begot Boaz by Rahab, Boaz begot Obed by Ruth, Obed begot Jesse, and Jesse begot David the king.*

We also know the Jesus Christ came through the lineage of King David. Rahab's life proves that it is not how you start that ultimately matters; it's how you finish. Be determined to finish well.

Speak the WORD

Speak this affirmation out loud as often as possible, based on this week's study:

> "God, I am grateful that I have no need to fear enemies. You are with me every step of the way and you fight for me. You prepare a table before me and I can rest, knowing that I am secure in your protection."

Aim For Change

Read Joshua 2 and Deuteronomy 20:4. Then answer the following questions.

1. Why do you think it was advantageous for the spies to seek out Rahab?

2. Once the King of Jericho found out that the spies had come to Rahab, how did she respond to the king's men questioning?

3. What reason did Rahab give the spies for helping them?

4. What risks did Rahab take in assisting the spies? What risks did Rahab take if she had *not* helped the spies?

5. What was the ultimate outcome to Rahab's decision to help the spies?

6. Think about a major risk you've taken in your life that turned out well. What would have happened if you didn't have the courage to take the risk?

7. Think about your life now. Are there any areas in your life that are calling you to be courageous? If so, seek the Lord's wisdom in the action you should take, confident that He will be with you.

Week 4: Courage in Saving Lives (Esther)

Focus Scripture

Yet who knows whether you have come to the kingdom for such a time as this?"

- Esther 4:14

Lesson Insight

Most of us have heard the story of Esther, known as *Hadassah* in the Hebrew language. Esther is one of only two women who had books name after them in the bible (*Ruth* being the other). The book of Esther is also unique in another aspect: It does not name *God* once.

And yet, God's providential hand is seen through the book. He orchestrated events in Esther's life so that she was in the right place at the right time. Because of her position of influence, she was able to save the entire Jewish race from destruction.

Like many heroines, Esther life had humble beginnings: Her cousin Mordecai had raised her after the death of both of her parents. However, through extraordinary circumstances described in Esther 2:1-18, Esther was made the queen of King Ahasuerus (Xerses) of Persia.

Soon after, Mordecai discovered a plot by two of the king's disgruntled eunuchs to kill the king. However, Mordecai informed Esther of the plot and she told the king in Mordecai's name. The plot was thwarted and the eunuchs put to death.

While Mordecai was looking out for the king's interests, a member of the king's staff, a man named Haman, was looking out for himself. The king had recently promoted Haman above the other princes and he was feeling self important. When Haman entered through the king's gate, all of the king's servants bowed and paid homage to him.

But Mordecai would not bow and pay homage to him. So in Haman's mind, Mordecai had to pay for the perceived insult.

However, Haman did not just want revenge on Mordecai; he had disdain for all of the Jews. He went to the king and told him that, because the Jews were disobedient to the king's laws, a decree should be written to order the destruction of the Jews.

King Ahasuerus apparently trusted Haman; the King told him to do to the Jews whatever seemed good to him. Haman ordered that on a certain day, all the Jews were to be killed - young and old, male and female.

Mordecai grieved when he heard about the evil decree. He told one of Esther's attending eunuchs to inform Esther. He also requested that Esther go to the king to intervene for the lives of their people. It should also be noted that the king was unaware that Esther herself was a Jew.

But Esther was in a bind; the law dictated that she could not go to the king unless summoned. If she dared to go to the king without being summoned, he could order her to be put to death...unless he showed mercy and held out the golden scepter to her.

When I read this, I wondered why Esther was concerned about the law in this regard; after all, she was the king's wife. Surely, he wouldn't put her to death for coming to see her husband! But then, a seemingly insignificant detail was mentioned in the account: Esther had not been summoned to the king for

30 days. That's a long time for a man and wife to be separated from one another.

Esther had no way of knowing what mood the king was in. She had no way of knowing if the reason he had not summoned her was because he was displeased with her. And if the king was displeased with her and she showed up in his court, death could be the result.

So, Esther explained the risk to her eunuch to relay to Mordecai. She may have thought that would have been the end of it. There was nothing she could do.

But she was wrong. Instead, Mordecai's response to her was one of indignation: "Do not think in your heart that you will escape in the king's palace any more than all the other Jews. For if you remain completely silent at this time, relief and deliverance will arise for the Jews from another place, but you and your father's house will perish. Yet who knows whether you have come to the kingdom for such a time as this? (Esther 4:13-14)"

Mordecai's last point is one for all of us to think about. You see, in Jeremiah 1:5, God told the prophet: "Before I formed you in the womb I knew you; Before you were born I sanctified you; I ordained you a prophet to the nations."

Do you think Jeremiah was special in this regard? No; before all of us were born, God had a purpose in mind for us too. He chose exactly the appointed time in which we were to be born into history; he has surely picked the time in which we will leave.

During the space between birth and death, God means for us to make a difference. And that is what Queen Esther ultimately decided to do.

She sent to Mordecai and told him to ask all the Jews to fast for three days and that she and her maids would also fast. I like Esther's final pronouncement: "And so I will go to the king, which is against the law; and if I perish, I perish!"

Most of us know the rest of the story (see Esther, chapters 5 - 8). Esther was accepted into court by the king and she invited the king and Haman to a banquet. There, Esther told the king how Haman had tried to have her and her people destroyed.

The plot that Haman had created to destroy the Jews destroyed him instead; the gallows that Haman had constructed to hang Mordecai upon were the very ones that he was hanged upon.

What about the king's original decree concerning the Jews? The king stated that once a decree was issued, he could not revoke it. However, he allowed a new decree to be written. This decree would allow the Jews to defend themselves using whatever means were necessary on the appointed day of destruction.

Because of Queen Esther's brave actions, the Jews were able to survive and go forth in joy and peace. When you exercise courage, you gain peace within yourself knowing that you did everything you could to make things right.

Plus, you enjoy the ultimate reward: A life with no regrets.

Speak the WORD

Speak this affirmation out loud as often as possible, based on this week's study:

> "God, thank you that you have appointed me to seek your kingdom for such a time as this. You said that your kingdom is righteousness, peace,

and joy in the Holy Spirit. Father, give me the courage to do what is right, knowing that if I do, peace and joy will ultimately follow."

Aim For Change

Read Esther, Chapters 3-8 and then answer the following questions.

1. Why did Haman plot to kill the Jews?

2. What did Mordecai ask Esther to do once he found out about the decree to destroy the Jews?

3. Why did Esther hesitate to do what Mordecai requested at first?

4. How did Mordecai appeal to Esther to get her to approach the king?

5. What was the final result of Esther's intervention?

6. If Esther had not had the courage to intervene, what would have likely happened?

7. Why do you think now is the best time for someone with your unique personality, talents,

abilities, and spiritual gifts to seek God's kingdom on this earth?

Study Summary

In the *Courageous Heart* bible study, you discovered that the bible documents how God empowered certain women to take the right actions at the right time to affect history.

Specifically, you learned about how four women demonstrated courage in tough situations: Abigail, Deborah, Rahab, and Esther.

Points to Remember

- Whenever you are faced with a situation in which courage is needed, take the time to consider the mightiness of your God. Remember that you are not alone. **Focus on your Father.**

- There is power in speaking the right words at the right time, especially when those words bring light into the lives of others.

- When we are in God, we have no need to fear enemies. He fights for us against our enemies and we can be secure in His protection.

- Before all of us were born, God had a purpose in mind for us. He chose exactly the appointed time in which we were to be born into history. We are not meant to just get by; we were put on Earth to make a difference.

About the Author

"Just wanted to again thank you for sharing your unique and engaging presentation to help us take back our temples! You were truly a blessing and I know that many were enlightened by what you shared."

- **Danese Turner, Turner Chapel AME, Marietta GA**

Kimberly Taylor is the creator of **Takebackyourtemple.com**, a website that inspires Christians to Spiritual, emotional, and physical health. She is the author of the ebook *Take Back Your Temple* and the books ***The Weight Loss Scriptures***, ***God's Word is Food***, and **many others**.

Once 240 pounds and a size 22, Kim lost 85 pounds through renewing her mind and taking action upon God's word. Her experience led her to establish the **Take Back Your Temple** website. "Take Back Your Temple" is a prayer that asks God to take control of your body and your life so He can use them for His purpose and agenda.

Kim's weight loss success story has been featured on CBN's *The 700 Club,* and in *Prevention Magazine*, *Essence Magazine*, *Charisma Magazine* and many other magazines and newspapers. She has also been interviewed on various radio programs.

Kim exhorts people of faith to become good stewards of all the resources God has given to them, including time, money, talents, and physical health. "I am passionate about empowering others to adopt healthy lifestyles so they can fulfill their God-given purpose," she says.

"My dream is for God's people to stand apart because we are healthy, prosperous and living the abundant life to which we are called. I want non-believers to look at us and want what we have: Spiritual, mental, and physical wholeness. Then when they ask us what we are doing differently, we can tell them about Jesus, the author and finisher of our faith."

Stay Connected

You can stay connected with Kimberly Taylor through the following channels:

Amazon Author Page

You can learn about all of Kimberly Taylor's books and eBooks available on Amazon.com at one convenient location: **https://www.amazon.com/author/kimberlyytaylor**

Take Back Your Temple website

Kimberly's website, **www.takebackyourtemple.com/** shares her testimony of deliverance from emotional overeating through the change God made in her heart and mind. Hundreds of free articles on the website encourage other Christians on the road to Spiritual, emotional, and physical health.

YouTube

Kimberly is creating a *Bible Study for Women* channel with videos that discuss her insights on women of the bible. The channel address is **http://www.youtube.com/user/BibleStudyforWomen1** (Available September 11, 2012)

Facebook

You can connect with Kimberly on Facebook at **http://www.facebook.com/takebackyourtemple**. She also moderates a secret Facebook support group comprised of believers who struggle with emotional eating and are working to change their health. Details on how to join the group are available at *takebackyourtemple.com*.

Twitter

Follow Kimberly on Twitter at **twitter.com/tbytkimberly**

Pinterest

You can view Kim's Pinterest boards at
http://pinterest.com/tbyt/

All paperback versions of the *Bible Study for Women* series were published through **CreateSpace**.

www.ingramcontent.com/pod-product-compliance
Lightning Source LLC
Chambersburg PA
CBHW060627030426
42337CB00018B/3243